LET'S LOOK AT CUBA

BY **Nikki Bruno Clapper**

CAPSTONE PRESS
a capstone imprint

Pebble Plus is published by Capstone Press,
1710 Roe Crest Drive, North Mankato, Minnesota 56003
www.mycapstone.com

Library of Congress Cataloging-in-Publication Data
Names: Clapper, Nikki Bruno, author.
Title: Let's look at Cuba / by Nikki Bruno Clapper.
Description: North Mankato, Minnesota : Capstone Press, [2018] | Series:
   Pebble plus. Let's look at coutnries | Includes bibliographical references
   and index. | Audience: Ages 5-8.
Identifiers: LCCN 2017037879 (print) | LCCN 2017038379 (ebook) | ISBN
   9781515799269 (eBook pdf) | ISBN 9781515799146 (hardcover) | ISBN
   9781515799207 (pbk.)
Subjects: LCSH: Cuba--Juvenile literature.
Classification: LCC F1758.5 (ebook) | LCC F1758.5 .C53 2018 (print) | DDC
   972.91--dc23
LC record available at https://lccn.loc.gov/2017037879

Editorial Credits
Juliette Peters, designer; Tracy Cummins, media researcher; Laura Manthe, production specialist

Photo Credits
Alamy: CHLOE HALL, 13; Getty Images: PAUL J. RICHARDS/AFP, 16-17, Scott Wallace, 10-11;
Shutterstock: akturer, 14, Daniela Constantinescu, 21, Felix Lipov, 22-23, 24, Globe Turner, 22 Top,
jakubtravelphoto, 6, javier gonzalez leyva, Cover Bottom, Johann Helgason, 8-9, Kamira, Cover
top, Lesinka372, 15, Magr, 19, marcin jucha, Cover Middle, Cover Back, nale, 4, Roxana Gonzalez, 7,
simonovstas, 1, Tupungato, 4-5, vvital, 3

Note to Parents and Teachers

The Let's Look at Countries set supports national curriculum standards for social studies related
to people, places, and culture. This book describes and illustrates Cuba. The images support early
readers in understanding the text. The repetition of words and phrases helps early readers learn
new words. This book also introduces early readers to subject-specific vocabulary words, which are
defined in the Glossary section. Early readers may need assistance to read some words and to use
the Table of Contents, Glossary, Read More, Internet Sites, Critical Thinking Questions, and Index
sections of the book.

Printed in the United States of America.
010774S18

TABLE OF CONTENTS

Where Is Cuba?

Cuba is the largest island in the Caribbean Sea. It is almost as big as the U.S. state of Pennsylvania. Cuba's capital is Havana.

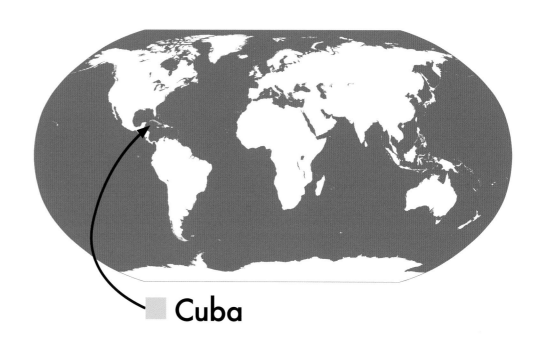

Cuba

From Beaches to Swamps

Beaches and grasslands cover most of Cuba. The country also has swamps and mountains. The air is hot and humid.

In the Wild

Cuban crocodiles live in swamps. Flamingos fly by beaches. Tiny hummingbirds feed on flowers. They are the size of your index finger.

Cuban crocodile

People

Most Cubans came

to the island from Spain.

Others are from Africa.

Asian people live

in Havana's Chinatown.

On the Job

Many Cubans work to help others. Some are tour guides or nurses. Other Cubans grow sugarcane or catch fish.

Let the Music Play

Cubans play salsa a lot. Salsa is a type of music and dance. It has a strong beat and high energy. Dancers twirl and twirl!

Play Ball!

Baseball is Cuba's main sport. Children play it on fields and city streets. The best players are on the national team.

At the Table

Cubans eat a lot of

pork, beans, and rice.

One main dish is shredded

beef with vegetables.

It is called *ropa vieja*.

ropa vieja

Famous Site

Old Havana is part
of Cuba's capital.
It has old churches, houses,
and plazas. Many buildings
are made of stone.

QUICK CUBA FACTS

Cuban flag

Name: Republic of Cuba

Capital: Havana

Other major cities: Santiago, Camagüey, Trinidad

Population: 30,741,062 (July 2016 estimate)

Size: 496,224 square miles (1,285,216 sq km)

Language: Spanish

Money: peso

GLOSSARY

capital—the city in a country where the government is based

humid—damp or moist

plaza—a public square or open space often used for ceremonies

sugarcane—a tall, tropical grass that has sugar in its woody stems

swamp—wet, spongy ground often partly covered by water

tour guide—a person who helps show visitors a country or place

READ MORE

Labrecque, Ellen. *Islands.* Learning About Landforms. Chicago: Heinemann-Raintree, 2014.

Moon, Walt K. *Let's Explore Cuba.* Let's Explore Countries. Minneapolis: Bumba Books, Lerner Publications, 2017.

Murray, Julie. *Cuba.* Explore the Countries. Minneapolis: ABDO Publishing Company, 2014.

INTERNET SITES

Use FactHound to find Internet sites related to this book.

Visit *www.facthound.com*

Just type 9781515799146 and go.

 **Super-cool stuff!** Check out projects, games and lots more at **www.capstonekids.com**

CRITICAL THINKING QUESTIONS

1. What are three things you would pack for a trip to Cuba?

2. Name a job some Cuban people have. What would you like or dislike about this job?

3. Why do you think Cubans are proud of Old Havana?

INDEX